Copyright

ISBN-13: 978-1985665293
ISBN-10: 1985665298

Disclaimer

This text is an informational guide. The material represents ideas, general teaching concepts, and health practices as summarized by Ms. Darbro. All data has been reviewed. Care should be taken when exercising in any situation. The publisher and the author are not responsible for errors, omissions or any consequences from application of the information in this text. The publisher and author make no guarantee or warranty, implied or express regarding details. A person's safety is their responsibility. Rely on yourself. Stay current. This text is not meant to replace the independent thought or judgment of individuals or instructors. Always seek advice from a professional when beginning or changing any program or program content. The author and publisher have made every effort to ensure the accuracy and validity of this text and all the material contained herein. Any use of this material is the sole risk of the reader. The author and publisher are not responsible for the application and use of any material contained in this text.

For more information contact Michelle Darbro at
www.wildcatdojo.com

Table of Contents

<u>Preface</u>

I wrote this self-defense book for everyone. If you train in a fighting art or if you have never considered that type of training, this book will make you ready and willing to defend your own life.

As my years in karate passed, I noticed that a very common statement from many students has been: I'm learning techniques, and I understand that the need to defend myself might come up. What I don't understand is how to put the knowledge together, to create my own safety net of self-defense.

On these pages, I have organized a simple, effective plan for self-defense. It is based on my experience as a martial artist, yet it is adaptable to any skill level, as long as the desire to understand is there.

I encourage everyone who reads this book to be ready for any, and all situations that may require self-defense. One good way to accomplish that is to leave this copy on your coffee table. That will allow you and your company to peruse it regularly and keep safety fresh in your memory.

Michelle Darbro
USA Goju Federation
2017

Introduction: Why Should I Read This Book

Karate Training / Self-Defense / Women at Risk

Does karate training apply to self-defense in reality? Yes! Can you learn to protect yourself if you don't train in karate? Absolutely! If you presently train in karate, your confidence should grow with each day of training. You ladies who are not formally training in karate can and should become capable and prepared to defend yourself. All of you must strengthen your confidence in your self-defense by increasing your proficiency in four areas.

Learn to:
1. Be Aware: Assess the level of danger and the necessity to use physical force.
2. Whenever possible, have a plan of action.
3. Execute the best technique available for the situation.
4. Consciously strengthen your will to act.

Each of these points will be defined below and reinforced within each chapter.

The Need for Physical Force

Which situations warrant the use of self-defense? The answer is obvious; any situation in which life is threatened. Examples include: a physical attack, kidnapping attempt, rape attempt, and home invasion. If the situation will result in death or permanent damage, the need for self-protection is undeniable.

Plan of Action

Your plan should be as simple as possible for self-preservation. Have the plan ready at all times. This will require that you pay attention to your surroundings. An argument that I hear, is that by encouraging a plan of action, I am encouraging people to live in fear. I believe the opposite is true. When an unexpected situation occurs, knowing the defenses available and how to apply them IS NOT living in fear; it is creating an empowered individual.

Techniques for Self-Defense

For the purposes of this text, I will use the term technique, to mean a set of moves designed to stop an attacker. A wide range of techniques is available to a trained martial artist. The range of sophistication is unlimited. Inside these pages, I will deal with reliable, direct technology. These techniques are applicable in almost any situation and are easy to remember whether or not you train in a fighting art.

The Will to Act

To be willing to act is to have your body actually move when you ask it to, rather than freeze up in fear, shock, tension or anxiety. When confronted with physically threatening situations, you will need to draw upon your inner strength: your *Chi*. An entire chapter is dedicated to this important asset.

The four components listed above when working together, will create the armor you need for self-protection and self-defense. You might even find that working toward strength in these areas will be fun!

> I believe these four parameters of self-defense will work for everyone; men, women, and children. This text, however, focuses on us – the women.

INTERACTIVE EXERCISE 1

1. Sit and consider your daily routine. Can you think of any parts of your routine that could use better safety precautions, awareness and readiness? List a few.

   ____

   ____

   ____

2. List situations that you have already thought of, where avoidance is a choice. (The answer to this question is inside of you, not in this text.)

   ____

   ____

   ____

3. Define (in your own words) the four components of a complete self-defense routine.
   Pay Attention ____
   Be Prepared. ____
   Memorize Techniques ____
   Willing to Take Action ______________________________________

CHAPTER 1
Situations That Require Self-Defense

The only situation that will require you to become violent is one where your life or the life of a loved one is threatened. The question I pose is this: Is fighting back an option for you? The choice to live fearfully, or be aware and ready, is yours and mine to make with each and every day.

Being prepared daily will require only one small skill: **Pay Attention!** I understand that this is difficult to remember all the time. Looking at life, really looking, each moment needs to become part of your routine. I want you to pay attention to the details of your everyday activities, so often that it becomes a life-saving habit.

When you are assessing which situations are life threatening there are two extremes. Waiting too long to recognize that danger is imminent is one mistake. The opposite, confronting every person with a bad attitude, is also fruitless. The calmness and confidence that training instills in you, will assist you in being able to differentiate between what angers you and what threatens you. One easy tip-off that trouble is near, is when the hairs on the back of your neck 'stand up'. My motto is; if it feels unsafe, act accordingly.

Wherever you are, whatever you are doing, awareness is the key to safety. In your home, away from it, driving, walking with friends or alone, an awareness of your surroundings and the proximity of potential danger are imperative to your well-being.

INTERACTIVE EXERCISE 2

1. What is worth fighting for?

   ____

   ____

   ____

2. Take a moment to think of the places and times within your day, that you might let your guard down and not take precautions for safety. List a few, and brainstorm ways to increase awareness at these times:

   ____

   ____

   ____

Safety Preparation

We'll take a lesson from the world of scouting and be prepared. Okay?

Around Your Home

Let's begin by assessing the area outside your home. I will start with some easy safety tips:

- Please don't hide a key under the mat. Here are a few ideas. Give a spare to a trusted neighbor or family member. If you insist on hiding one, be inventive about where you hide it and change locations after each use.
- Keep the bushes by your doors cut back so no one can hide waiting for you.
- Thorny bushes are also a deterrent.
- Talk to your neighbors. It is safer when we watch out for each other.
- Don't advertise if you live alone. Use your first initial on your mailbox and correspondence. If you have a landline listing, request the first initial there, also.

> Remember, it isn't necessary to be best friends with everyone on your street. However, if an emergency arises, it will help if you know each other. When possible, take just a minute to make that happen.

Inside Your Home

How many times have people reminded you to keep your doors locked when you are inside the house? How often have you walked over and noticed it wasn't locked? For me, it is countless. (*And I teach it!*) Bolt locks are an excellent tool for keeping out intruders. All hardware stores carry them, and they are easy to install. Another simple precaution that we've been told many times is the peephole in your door. It is another must have safety measure.

- Do I need to remind you NOT to open the door to strangers?
- When people seem official, check validity. All adults today should appreciate this precaution – even police.
- Understand what objects by your door can be used as weapons. (*I keep a spray can and flashlight at every door…just in case!*)
- Slow down and think, rather than reacting or becoming thoughtless when considering opening the door to strangers.

Other openings, windows and glass doors, should also be kept secure against a potential attacker. This seems so logical, it should go without saying. Use the necessary precautions at all entranceways into your home.

Traveling from the doorways to the interior of your home, there are more details to consider. I encourage you to keep your landline. In fact, I'd like you to have a phone connected to it that doesn't need electricity. This line might bring help when there is no cell phone signal.

Understanding the layout of your home and the location of key things will be an asset if you have an intruder. Remember what escape options could be used in an emergency. Then, if need be, the plan is simple; run to a neighbor and get help.

As we do when outside, we all have to learn to pay attention to details. When entering, notice if something is not the way you left it. The key is to be in the moment and paying attention. If you open your door and get an uneasy feeling, take the course of action you think best.

> There is so much to remember daily. This transition takes time. When mapping out your self-defense plan, make small changes and try to keep the changes. Then you can build a strong foundation.

Would you like to:
- Leave and get help?
- Call someone while staying close by?
- Enter at your own risk (taking precautions along the way, of course)!
  It is a great idea to think about this in advance. That way you will have a plan of action!

May I suggest that you spend some time considering "what if". What if I came home and the front door was left opened? What if I entered my house and noticed things were moved around? What would be my best plan? I call this the - What If Game -. You can think about it when you're sitting in a line somewhere. You can also talk about it with friends and workout partners. Playing this game will help you have a plan. Having a plan builds confidence. Finally, confidence will lead you to take action in an emergency.

If the situation were to dictate that escape was not an option, I want you to know everything you can to defend yourself inside your home. Think about what household items can be used as weapons. The list is endless. Here are a few:

- Pans and cooking utensils
- Spray cans
- Flashlights to blind them
- Table lamps
- All sharp objects
- All bric-a-brac

Be inventive when you look around your home. Everything has potential.

You'll be happy to know that it is easy to include and inform children of safety precautions. Obviously, children of different ages require different strategies. If your children are babies, they are physically near you most of the time. If you can take them and get out, that is the best answer. If not, you will need to use your knowledge, technique and courage to thwart the attack. (Don't worry. Plenty of fighting techniques are included in this text.) With older children, a conversation about personal safety should be as common as a conversation about fire safety.

- Assure them that there is nothing to fear.
- Remind them that knowledge of self-defense is power.
- Take opportunities to review self-defense techniques.
- Keep a calm and confident tone of voice.

If you are uncomfortable having this conversation, find a self-defense program in your area. Classes should be available through the police department and through local karate schools. The youngest students I've trained are just over three years old. We make a game of the techniques. During the game, we discuss details about what a bad guy would be like, and what to do if we see one. Everyone has fun and feels empowered.

There are a few precautions inside the home that you can implement to further your child's readiness. Look over this list and see what works for you.

Safety inside the Home at a Glance:
1. Landlines on every floor.
2. Doors and windows secured.
3. Knowledge of emergency escapes.
4. Knowledge of potential weapons inside the home.

- Is an intercom system workable in your home?
- At least have code words that mean emergency and run.
- As stated earlier, planning and practice help.

Finally, and very importantly, don't underestimate your children's ability; or your own! All the techniques in this book will work for young and old, both outside and inside. I encourage you to create regular opportunities to review self-defense techniques with the kids. Run, yell, laugh, and keep it fun. While you're having fun, you're instilling a safety action in yourself and your children. Although I hope you never need it, it will be instinctual if you do!

INTERACTIVE EXERCISE 3

1. List at least three ways to keep the outside of your home safe.

   ____

   ____

   ____

2. Now list at least three ways to keep the inside of your home safe.

   ____

   ____

   ____

3. Think, talk, or write about what your plan will be if you come home to an intruder.

   ____

   ____

   ____

4. List one household item in each room of your home that could be used as a weapon, if the need arises.

   ____

   ____

   ____

5. Name at least one way to empower your children in self-defense awareness.

   ____

   ____

   ____

Safety Away From Home

Now that I have established the idea of awareness, application outside the home should be easy. I like to call my strategy "Appreciating the Day". Look around. What do you see? When leaving the house, look around. Are there unusual cars on your block? Don't be shy to call the local police if a car is sitting near your home and it doesn't belong there. *(I have used this strategy. I called the non-emergency number. The sheriff came and it turned out that the car – which had been there for 2 days – was a realtor. The realtor was a little bothered. But the sheriff was glad to check it out for me!)*

As you travel through your days, keep the wonderful viewing of nature (and people) in your thoughts and actions. Look around when you arrive at home, and before getting out of the car. You will be pleasantly surprised at the things you'll see. Nature is beautiful and occasionally, neighbors change their yard, car, or even the color of the house. It is vastly more interesting to be in the moment, seeing and appreciating, than to be caught in your own thoughts while simultaneously creating a less safe environment.

Common sense safety will be the same no matter when or where you are located. Let's look at two different situations:

<table>
<tr><td>

Walking
1. **Pay Attention.**
2. **Plan.**
3. **Be ready to implement your plan.**
4. **Walk facing traffic. This makes it difficult for an attacker to drag you into their car.**

How to test if you're being followed:
- **Cross the street.**
- **If the person crosses the street, cross back.**
- **If they cross back, chances are, they're following you.**
- **Go to the nearest public place. Use your phone to get help.**

</td><td>

Traveling
1. **Pay Attention**
2. **Plan**
3. **Be ready to implement your plan.**
4. **Don't advertise it if you are traveling alone.**

Inside the hotel:
- **Check out the room thoroughly when you arrive.**
- **Keep doors locked and use the peephole.**
- **Obviously, don't open the door to strangers. Check with the desk if hotel staff knock uninvited.**
- **Take advantage of the Do Not Disturb sign.**

</td></tr>
</table>

If you are traveling with children, you want to follow the precautions you follow at home. Communicate; teach your children from a young age to keep their eyes and ears open. Doing that is the first step to living safely. Younger children will be with you in strollers, and carriers. Older children can and should be spoken to, clearly, lovingly, and honestly about everything, from strangers to the importance of keeping in contact.

One more tip, for those of you who love to walk. Here is the way to check to see if someone is following you on foot. First, cross the street. If the person crosses the street, cross back again. If they cross back – they're with you! As soon as you realize you're being followed, take proper precautions. Call someone on your cell. Go into a crowded place and ask for assistance. I do not suggest confrontation. It isn't necessary. (*I was followed once in an antique district. This was before cell phones. I went into a business and called the non-emergency number. When the police drove over, the potential attacker left. It was very simple to stay safe that day.*)

With each section of this text, I'm attempting to add on to your awareness and self-responsibility. I hope you are gaining confidence with this added knowledge.

Safety in the Car

With a few adaptations, safety while driving will be as easy as at home. Attention to detail and an awareness of your surroundings will hopefully become part of your daily routine. There are 3 areas in driving that deserve our attention: what we leave inside the car when we get out of it, if we're sitting in the car waiting or doing work, and finally while the car is in motion.

The first one is easy. My motto to live by is: "Don't leave it in the car unless you're willing to lose it." This motto has made me rethink everything from what I carry in my purse to the true value of something I am about to leave in my car. (Think laptop). It is eye opening to think about this daily. Try it!

These next two situations, I'll put in bullet form for ease of reading and ease of memory.

<table>
<tr><td valign="top">

Safety While Driving
1. Doors locked.
2. Windows up.
3. When possible, don't go alone.
4. If going alone, please tell someone your plans!
5. As always, pay attention. Especially at intersections.
6. Place your purse in a place that isn't obvious.
7. Keep your cell phone charged.
8. Be aware of objects within reach you could use to thwart an attacker.

</td><td valign="top">

Safety When Parked
1. Doors locked.
2. Windows up when possible.
3. Pay Attention to your surroundings!
4. Find as safe a place to park as possible, of course.
5. Keep weapons handy.

</td></tr>
</table>

More bullets for car safety can be found in the next chapter.

INTERACTIVE EXERCISE 4

1. Is self-defense outside the home very different than inside the home? Discuss.

   ____

   ____

2. Think of at least 2 safety precautions that you can use while traveling.

   ____

   ____

3. Think of the different stages of self-defense for your children. What applies at what age? Make a few notes for the future:

   ____

   ____

4. Phone a friend and discuss some of the ideas we've covered.

CHAPTER 2
Have a Plan

I'd like you to have a strategy for your day to day life. As a martial artist, my philosophy has always been that to act will be more effective than to react. In order to have a plan, you'll need to think ahead. The more you consider what you can do in different emergency scenarios, the more empowered you will continue to feel.

First, let's revisit the world of common sense. I cannot emphasize enough the importance of these next few pages.

You Brain is Your Best Weapon

I'd like to challenge you. Think about safety more and trivia less. That is the challenge. The concept is simple. Make a concerted effort to live a life of common sense safety. Although I've stated it earlier, here it is again:

- Pay Attention. This will be the biggest deterrent to becoming a victim.
- Travel, even locally, prepared. Charge your phone. Have proper directions. Have gas in the car.
- Tell friends or family where you are going and when you'll return.
- Be wary of strangers. Follow the advice we give our children. Using the ideas below, don't let a stranger invade your personal space. More importantly, don't wander, unaware, into his.

We know these well. Now let's create routines based on them.

Say What You Mean and Mean What You Say

Let's look at that sentence in two parts. First, what does it mean to "say what you mean?" One of the biggest mistakes I think many women make is to choose having a courteous manner over clarity of words, tone and voice. When a person approaches, use clear, plain language. If the person is coming too close to you, say exactly that. If you want the person to leave you alone, say that.

Compare these two responses:

Someone approaches and begins a conversation. You turn to walk away and he follows. You say "I'd rather be alone right now." Or you say, "You are too close; please back up now." One is more courteous, but the other is clear. In the first sentence, the person can respond with more talk while continuing to get closer to you. In the second sentence, if the person does not back up, you will immediately know that more action is necessary.

Now let's finish with a look at the other half of the sentence. What does "and mean what you say." actually mean?

If you tell a stranger, "If you come any closer, I am going to scream." and then you don't scream, you are creating a bigger problem. My philosophy is Not to say, "I am going to scream." I just do it! However, if you say "I'm going to scream." - Please scream! Scream as loudly and as insanely as possible.

If someone gets close to you, speak up. The choice of words is yours. Say "YOU ARE TOO CLOSE; BACK UP." Or say "QUIT MOVING. BACK UP." Avoid sentences that are long or that contain an if/then consequence. If the person continues to move toward you, use one of the four defense strategies listed here:

- Be visible. Make people aware that you are in trouble.
- Use sound devices: a whistle, a car's panic mode.
- Scream "STRANGER" or some other word.
- If you are getting the feeling that this person is truly a danger (rather than just dense and pushy), hit them. (See the chapter on techniques.) After hitting, RUN for help.

As a woman, usually smaller than your attacker, learn to trust your intuition. If something feels wrong, it probably is. Be prepared to think on your feet. If someone is pressuring you to do something your intuition tells you not to do – follow your instincts.

One more quick note: If a car stops and asks for directions, be courteous but keep your distance. Stay aware that attackers come in all shapes, sizes, ages and genders.

> **Quick List on How to Use Your Voice**
> **As a Weapon**
> 1. Scream (Overcome all obstacles and let the sound come out).
> 2. Lie (Tell strangers you are contagious, act delirious "I see ghosts.")
> 3. Say what you mean and mean what you say.

The Best Way to Get Out of Trouble is to Stay Out of Trouble

Be Alert and Be Aware. By now you may be thinking that I have said the same thing too many times. The importance of common sense awareness cannot be overstated. Most days are busy and hectic. This doesn't leave a lot of time for awareness. With a little effort, you can change that. Here is a list to review often and tell yourself truthfully: Are you remembering to do these things regularly?

- When you leave your home, look around.
- Repeat this process when arriving home.
- Walk tall and pay attention at all times.
- Keep arms and legs free enough to use. Please don't overload your arms with packages.
- Stay aware of the distraction of cell phones. Please don't get so involved in your phone call that you become unaware of your surroundings.

I love the idea of looking around no matter where I am. I've begun to notice how much beauty surrounds me and it reminds me to be grateful for nature's beauty. Everything that I have been talking about, and will continue to talk about, is easy to do and easy to forget to do. My goal is to use this text to keep these ideas in the forefront of your thoughts.

INTERACTIVE EXERCISE 5

1. What is your most important weapon?

   ____

   ____

   ____

2. Define "Say what you mean and mean what you say."

   ____

   ____

   ____

3. Discuss ways to make common sense safety a part of your daily life. Include places and times we might forget to implement these ideas.

   ____

   ____

   ____

Keys and Other Devices for Defense

Make a point of having something in your hand that can be used as a weapon if needed. One option is your car keys. You'll notice in the photo below, that I want you to hold the keys vertically. Place one key in between each finger. This can be used to rake down the face of an attacker.

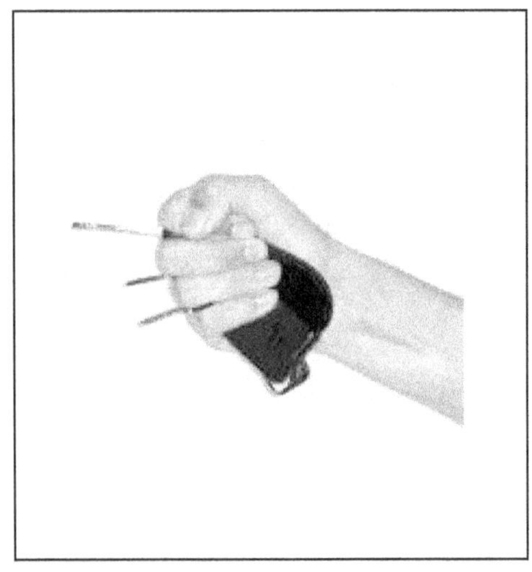

How to Hold Your Keys

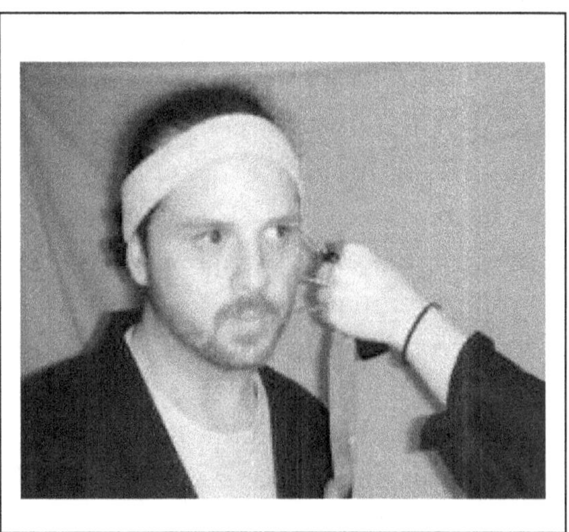

How to Rake the Face

There is a small device sold online and in Martial Arts stores. It is called a *yawara* stick. You carry it on your keychain. *Yawara* sticks are made of wood, plastic, and metal. When you wrap your hand around the stick, you can use it to poke the temples, eyes, throat, and nose of the attacker. Devices like a set of keys or a *yawara* stick serve to make a smaller hand into a more powerful striking implement, sometimes referred to as a "power pack".

Let's finish by mentioning the small aerosol cans of pepper or mace. This is a good deterrent as well. (*I don't use this device for two reasons. One, it is labor intensive to retrieve it from its packet. And two, I'd have to focus on which way the spray was going so it didn't end up accidentally spraying me.*) Please make your own decision when choosing which device will best suit your needs.

Here is a table of everyday items that can be used for self-defense. Use my list as a start, but see every item in your daily life with the potential to become a tool for defending your own life.

The Tool	Where to Hit	The Tool	Where to Hit
Nail File Cork Screw Pencil / Pen	Poke eyes, throat, or ears. Another use is in the soft tissue near the collar bone.	Book Purse Jewelry	Throw these and run.
Purse Belt and Buckle	Swing it at the face, neck, shoulders, or groin.	Umbrella Cane	Strike the legs, feet, and groin.
		Car Door or Window	These can be used to hit outward, or catch the body when slammed.

How to Plan for Driving

There are things we can plan for, where car travel is concerned. Think, talk with family and make a plan for these contingencies:

- When driving, where to set your purse. Out of sight is better than setting it on the front passenger seat.
- If someone tries to enter the car while you're in it with the engine running, are you willing to drive away? This is something to consider before the need arises.
- In recent times, people will tap your bumper. When you get out to assess the damage, they rob you. This is another reason NOT to let your guard down when you are sitting at an intersection. Give up valuables to save your life. Get as many details as you can for the authorities.

- What is your plan if your car breaks down? There are many choices. Obviously, call for help. Stay in the car. If people stop to help, tell them you have help on the way. If you decide to get out of the car, try to have one of the weapons we've discussed in your hand. Don't take your eyes off the person who has generously volunteered to help. Let them lift the tire out of a compartment etc.
- If you decide to walk for help, walk facing traffic. It makes you less vulnerable if someone drives up beside you and tries to pull you into their car.
- Here are some suggestions on what to do if someone tries to enter the car while you're in it:
  - a.) Slide out of the passenger seat and run for help.
  - b.) If the car is running, drive away!
  - c.) Scream, hit, try to use the door as a weapon.
  - d.) Pretend to be mute, sick, or crazy.

What to do if You are Being Followed in Your Car

1. Test if you are being followed by making a few random turns, changing your usual driving pattern.
2. If you think you are being followed, drive to a police station or fire station.
3. Call 911 as you drive and tell them of the emergency.

(I have used this method, without the 911. As soon as I turned into the Police Station, the person quit following me.)

As I have stated many times, it will be best if you think a little about these ideas in advance and Have A Plan.

INTERACTIVE EXERCISE 6

1. List your favorite defensive strategies while driving.

   ____

   ____

   ____

2. Name 3 common mistakes people make while they wait in a parked car.

   ____

   ____

   ____

3. Explain to a friend the danger of walking in the same direction as traffic is moving.

   ____

   ____

   ____

4. Play "what if" with these situations:
   a.) An attacker grabs your arm as you are getting in your car. You have your purse on your other arm. What do you do?
   b.) You drive into your driveway, and for the second day you notice a car across the street that you don't recognize with a man seated inside.
   c.) A stranger bumps your car with his, just two blocks from your home.

Special Circumstances

A few situations might unfold that could require specialized training and will call for individual adaptation of your knowledge. Those situations include being threatened with a weapon (knife or gun), being stalked, or being the victim of a carjacking. Although, I will touch on each one of these in this text, I suggest that you do more research on these dangerous topics. Everything is available on line. However, I like a great book on the subject. Also, if you train, talk to your teacher or coach.

Threatened by a Knife or a Gun

Here I am faced with discussing an area wrought with unpredictability. Those of you who are active in a karate training program have some experience in knife and gun defense. Hopefully, you are taking the time to think about how to apply your dojo training to your personal real life actions. These very dangerous moments will call for you to be courageous, inventive, and willful. If available, ask your instructor to have a class on individualized strategies against an armed attacker based on your size, strength and ability.

If no self-defense teacher is available, you will need to think for yourself. It is not possible for me to properly coach you in book format. Here are some ideas, but keep in mind every situation is different and will require you to adapt to the situation to overcome the threat.

Against a Knife	Against a Gun
1. Give up possessions the attacker is asking you to give up. 2. Throw your money or wallet to the side forcing them to look away – run. 3. Take off your jacket, throw it in their face and run. 4. Negotiate (talk) and move until you are in a position to run or be seen by others. 5. If you're at the car, use it. Use the door or the whole car.	Use the same 5 ideas just stated for the knife threat with the added danger, that when running, you need to make yourself a difficult target by moving in a wild zig-zag pattern. I truly hope you never have to use this advice.

It would be beneficial to learn some basic gun and knife defense. Spending time with these implements in your hands will lessen the distracting fear if it ever happens. At least you'll have a little experience. Check your local law enforcement establishments for courses in self-defense and gun safety.

Stalking

This seemingly obscure crime is terrifying. If you find yourself in this situation, contact the National Center for Victims of Crime (www.ncvc.org). There you will find an abundance of information directly related to stalking: what to do and how to help yourself.
Here is a short list of their advice:
- Do report the stalking right away and start proceedings to restrain the stalker.
- Do seek help through ncvc.org.
- DO NOT make contact with the stalker.

ANY contact with your stalker, even negative, will feed his obsession. No matter how much you want to tell him to "go to hell", NO contact is the best response.

Carjacking

Defense against this horrible crime hinges on being aware throughout the entire day. I'm sure that somewhere, sometime, a person will be carjacked after taking every precaution. But, let's take every precaution anyway. Just because we can…and remember…slowing down and looking at each moment of the day might just make your day more enjoyable and more memorable. Carjacking is almost always a crime of opportunity. So clearly, simple precautions are:
- Don't walk away from your car with the motor running.
- Don't walk away from the car with the keys in the ignition.

And finally, and most importantly:
- Please, don't EVER leave ANYTHING in the car (especially our children) that you are not willing to lose.

In this way we are doing our best to thwart this horrible crime of opportunity.
I like to say to myself: *Arrive a little late and alive instead of hurrying and through a lack of being in the moment, lose things that are important to me. SLOW DOWN."*

Having reviewed precautions, let's discuss what to do if you are not in the car when it is taken. Call the police. If the choice exists to follow at a distance, that might work. If you have anything in the car you can use to track the car – that is great.

If, however, you are IN the car you will need to think quickly. Here are some non-violent choices.
- Get out the passenger's side and follow the above advice.
- Pretend to faint, throw up or pretend to be completely crazy.

Any pretense will require you to carry on with the ruse. This is challenging. Thinking ahead what you might be willing to do, and practicing, will be beneficial.

Dating in the Modern World

Dating advice is no longer just for our children. We're all dating at all ages and in many different circumstances. Here is some simple precautionary advice:

- Keep personal information personal for as long as possible. Even your last name can remain private if possible.
- Meet first dates in public places. First dates do not need to know where you live.
- Tell friends or family where you are going, when you will return, and any information you have about your date.
- Carry a phone and cash for emergencies.
- Keep a few items in your purse that can be used for self-defense: keys, a pen, a small spray bottle.

Up to this point, there is so much information in this workbook. However, I can sum it up for you here:

- Live in the moment.
- Focus on what is actually in front of you.
- Use common sense and common courtesy in daily life.
- Play "what if" for different emergencies – planning a strategy to save your own life.
- Keep this book somewhere where you'll see it now and then, reminding you of how important this will be, if you need it.

INTERACTIVE EXERCISE 7

1. The number or website of a gun safety course in your area is:

    ____

2. True or False: Acknowledging a stalker will fuel his behavior.

    ____

3. List 2 actions you should take if you think you are being stalked:

    ____
    ____
    ____

4. List conclusions that have meaning from the text so far. What do you want to remember?

    ____
    ____
    ____

CHAPTER 3
Techniques That Could Save Your Life

In this chapter, I will detail the sequence of events involved in a physical confrontation. Practicing and preparing to fight back does not have to be a full time occupation. There are simple concepts that are easy to practice, easy to remember, and useful in saving your own life.

Every dangerous situation cannot be imagined. However, please remember that some forethought of potentially dangerous situations will create some emergency strategies that you can always follow. As I have previously stated, to achieve this level of preparedness use your imagination and create a plan for imaginable vulnerable situations.

One step you can take to bolster your preparedness, involves understanding hitting and being hit. If you are not presently in a martial arts program, find a club or a teacher that will throw strikes at you. This will create a person who is less distracted by the physicality of someone coming at you in life. You will be able to learn how to block, while strengthening your body and your spirit.

Now it is time to move our bodies, implement our plan. It will be easy to remember what I suggest that you do, because the plan is always the same.

1. **Distract your attacker by <u>talking</u>. Use your voice as a weapon. You can ask questions, babble incoherently or even scream like Tarzan!**
2. **<u>Hit</u>. Hit and be accurate. Read the target chart on the next page to get started on where and how to hit.**
3. **<u>Run</u>. Don't look back. Don't try to prove anything. Get out of there and get some help.**

This three part recipe is based on the simple fight – flight pattern that we are all born with. Modern communication has allowed that negotiate is also a choice. My idea is that if a life threatening situation were to happen, we should use all three choices in the specific order recommended.

Keep this three-part recipe in mind as I show you the moves of each technique.

<table>
<tr><td>
Remember
The actions of thinking ahead, planning and imagining what you will do will fortify your spirit. These actions will strengthen your confidence and lessen the fear that could paralyze you in an emergency.
</td><td>
And:
1. Talk
2. Hit
3. Run
</td></tr>
</table>

Where to Hit

	Targets	Use this Strike
Breathing	Temples	Hammerfist Pencil
	Eyes	Thumb Fingers Keys Pencil
	Nose	Palm Heel Hammerfist
	Throat	Hammerfist Elbow Web of the hand Edge of hand
Shock Absorbers	Groin	Shin bone Knee Fist Cane Umbrella
	Front or side of Knees	Foot Umbrella Stick
	Rear of Knee	Foot Umbrella Stick
	Instep	Heel Stick

The areas on the body that you should attack when defending yourself are the Brains, Breathing and (what we call) Shock Absorbers – the lower carriage of the body. Memorize our chart and pick your favorite attack targets. This plan will lead to the most successful outcome in a confrontation.

The following pages contain close up photos of our recommended target areas. Review these pictures often and practice.

Brains THE TEMPLES

Hammerfist to the Temple

Using your fist as a
hammer is effective.

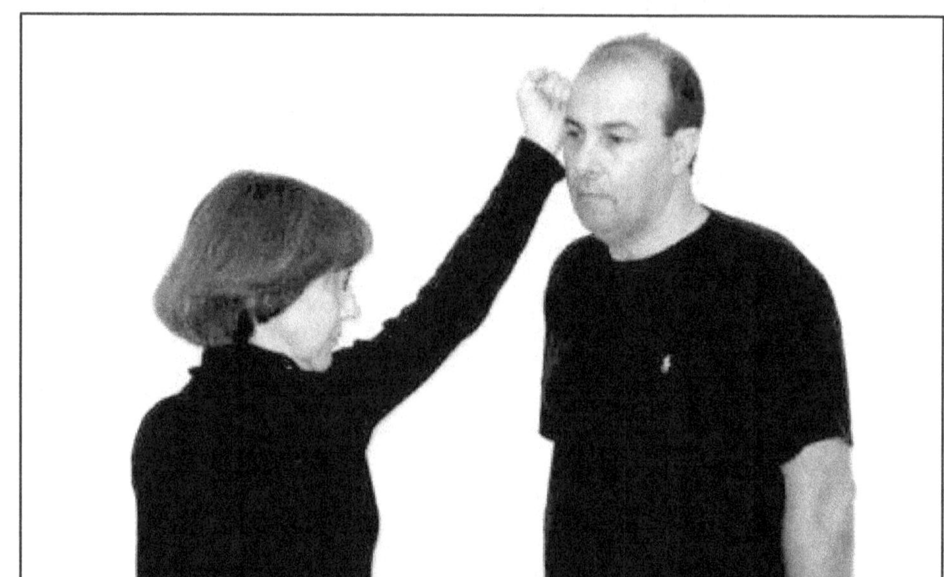

Pen to the Temple

If you have a small
object in hand, it
can be used

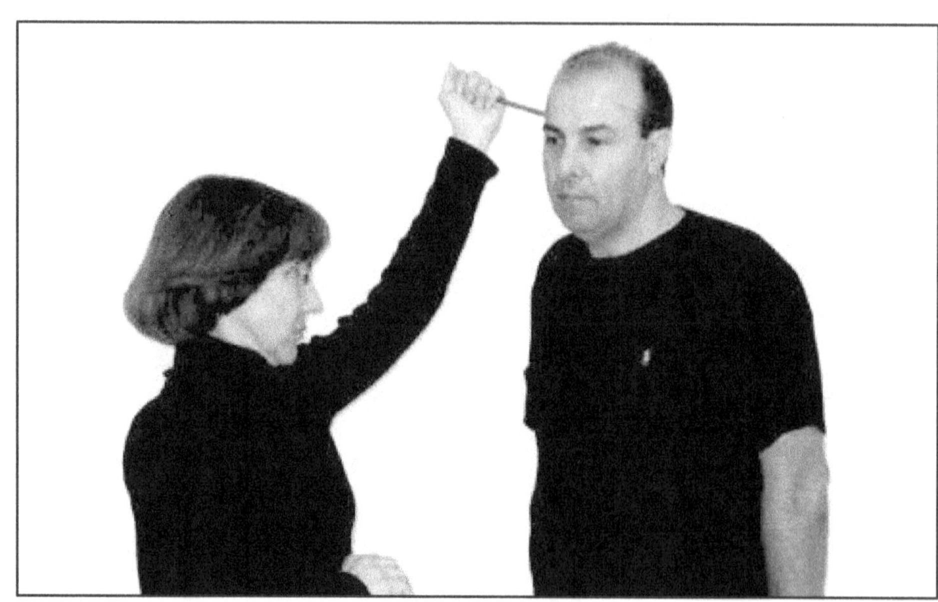

Brains THE EYES

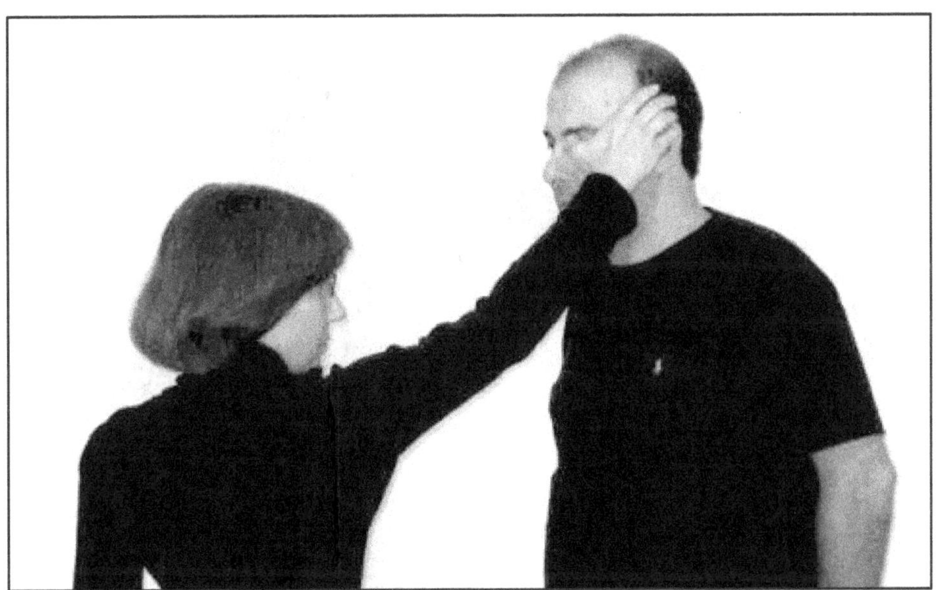

This strike seems drastic, but it could save your life.

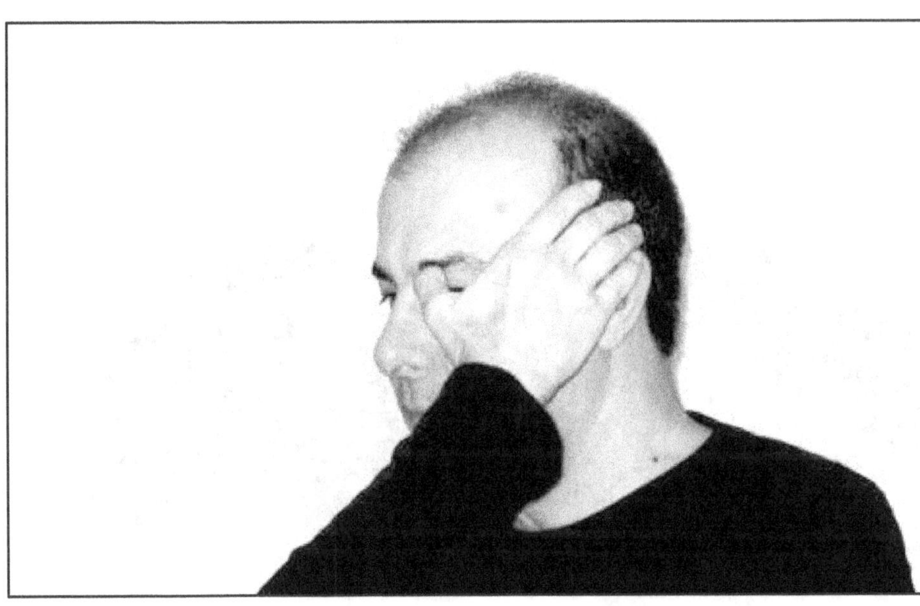

Here you can see the damage possible. When the attacker is close to you   (and he will be), this strike is perfect.

Brains THE EYES

Fingers in the Eyes

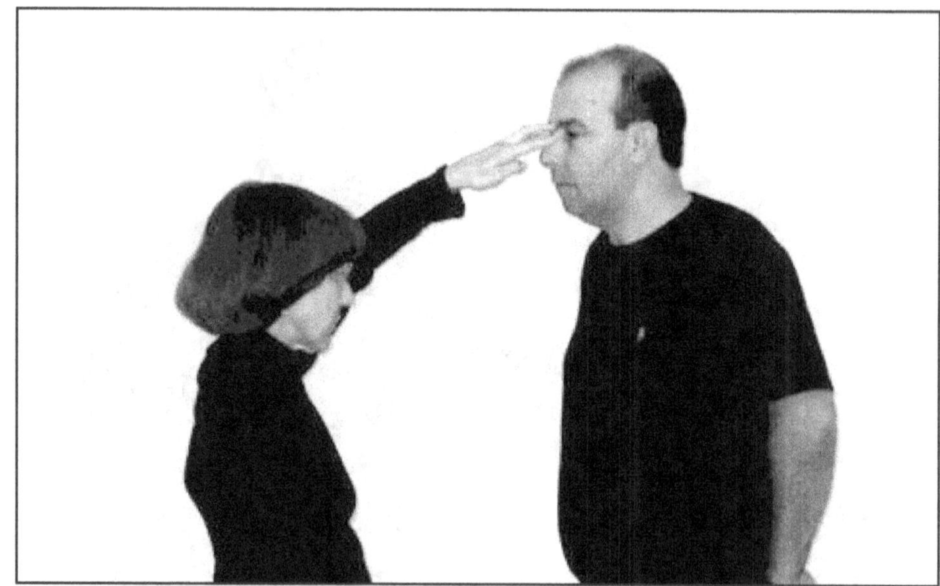

When using the fingers, strike hard and fast like a snake.

A Closer Look

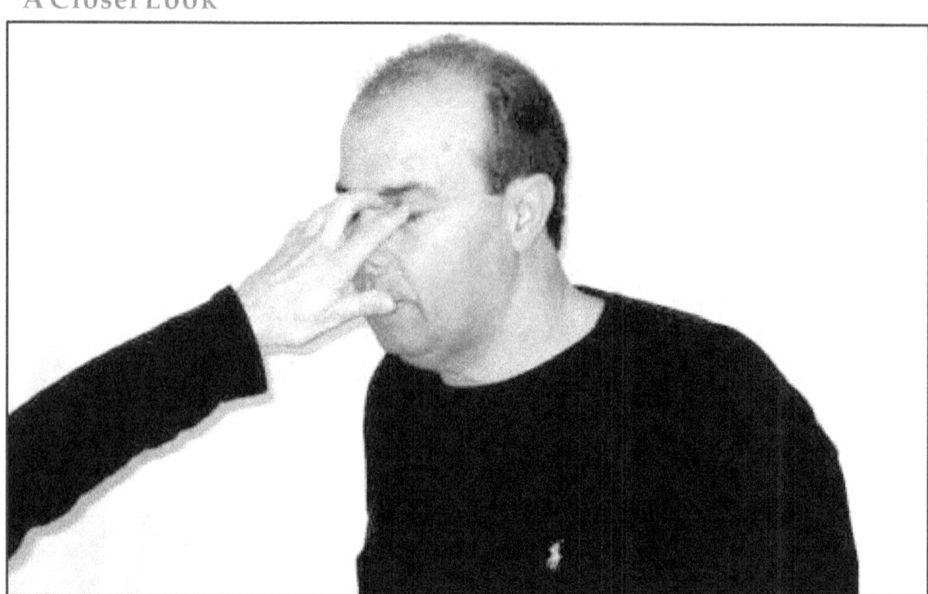

Keep your fingers taunt when delivering this strike.

Brains THE EYES

Keys to the Eyes

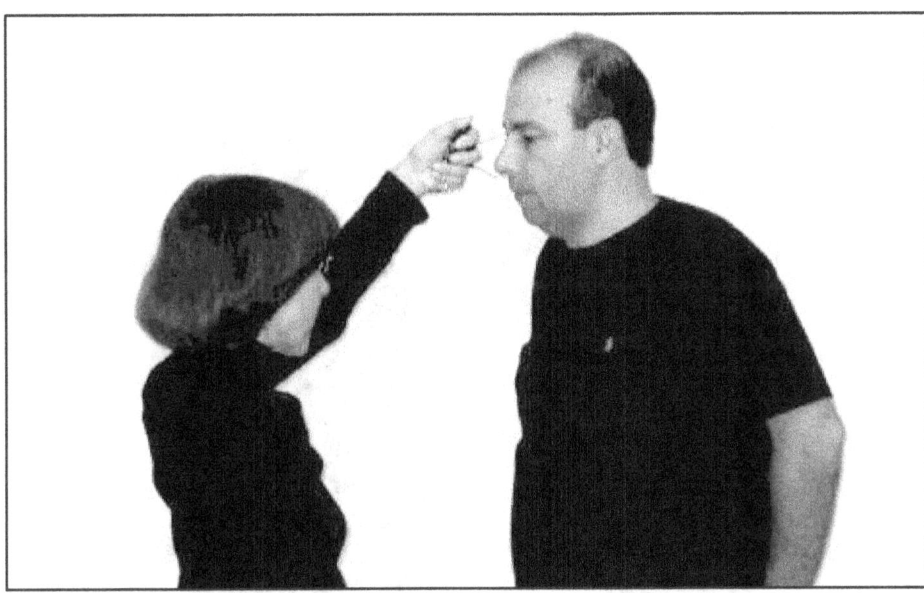

Rake downward against the eyes and skin. If you use a keyless entry system, the remote can dangle loosely from your fist.

A Closer Look

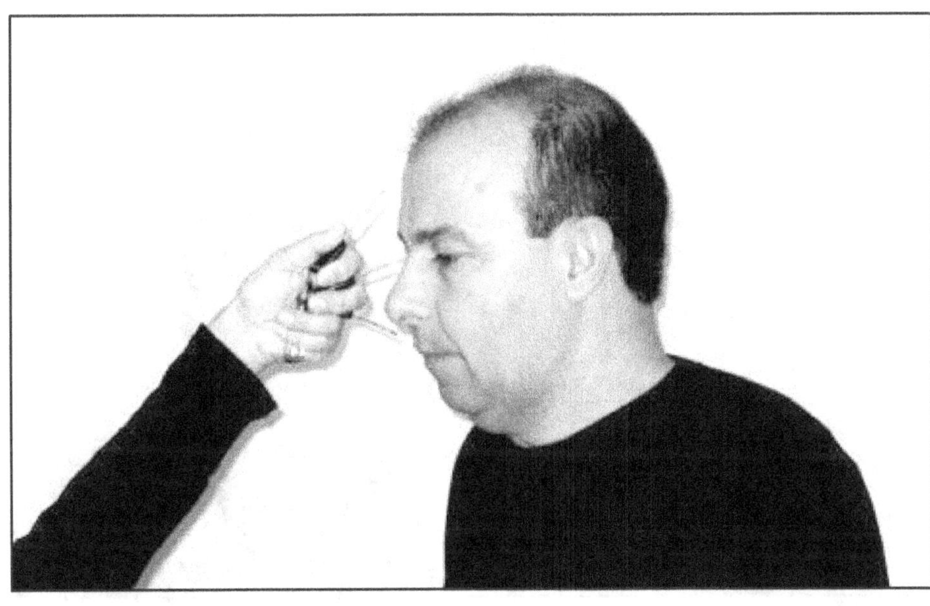

As shown here, hold the keys vertically between the second and third knuckles.

Brains THE EYES

Pen or Pencil to the Eyes

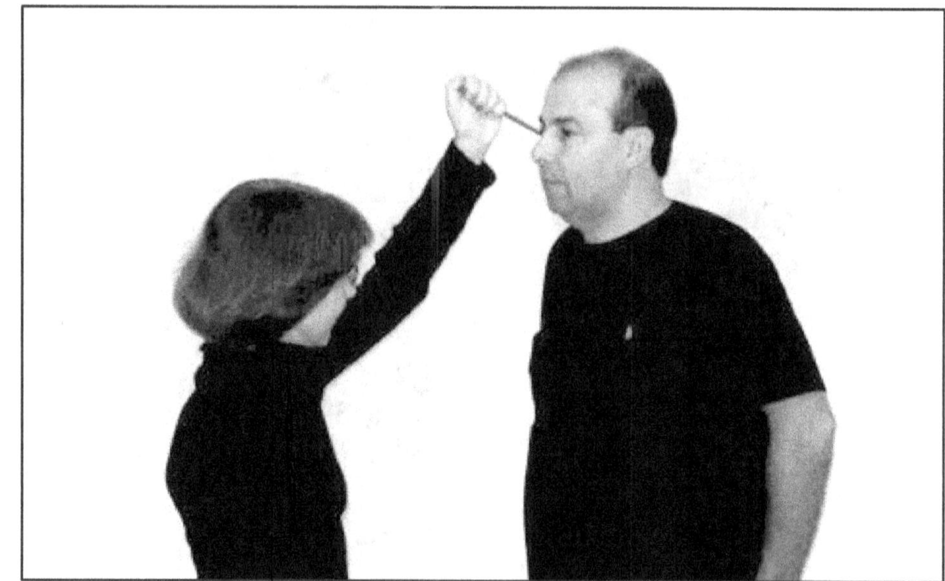

A pen or pencil is
easy to carry,
increases your
reach by six inches,
and can penetrate.

A Closer Look

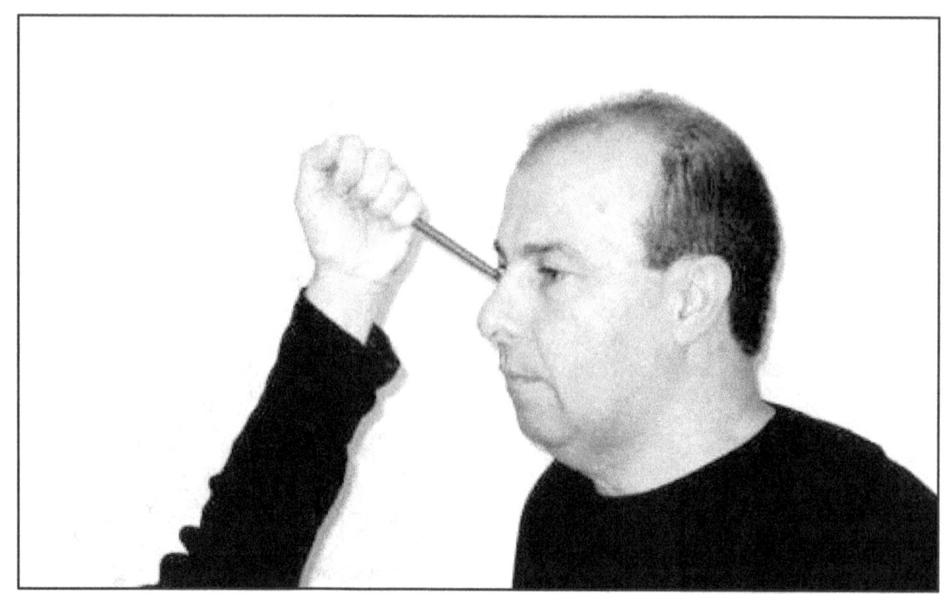

By now
I hope you
understand what
an effective and
vulnerable target
the eyes are.

Breathing THE NOSE

Palm Heel to the Nose

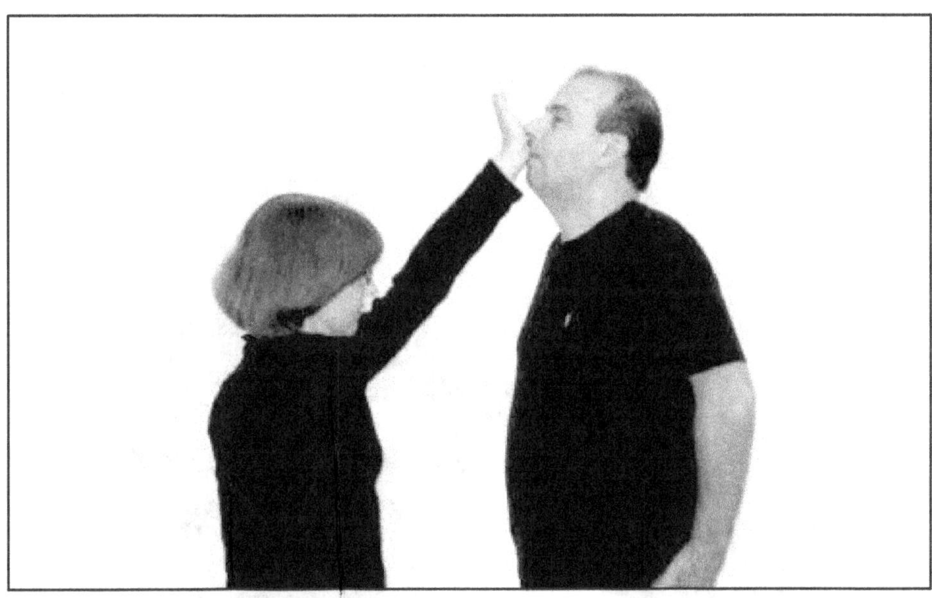

Hitting the nose attacks both the breathing and the brains.

Hammerfist to the Nose

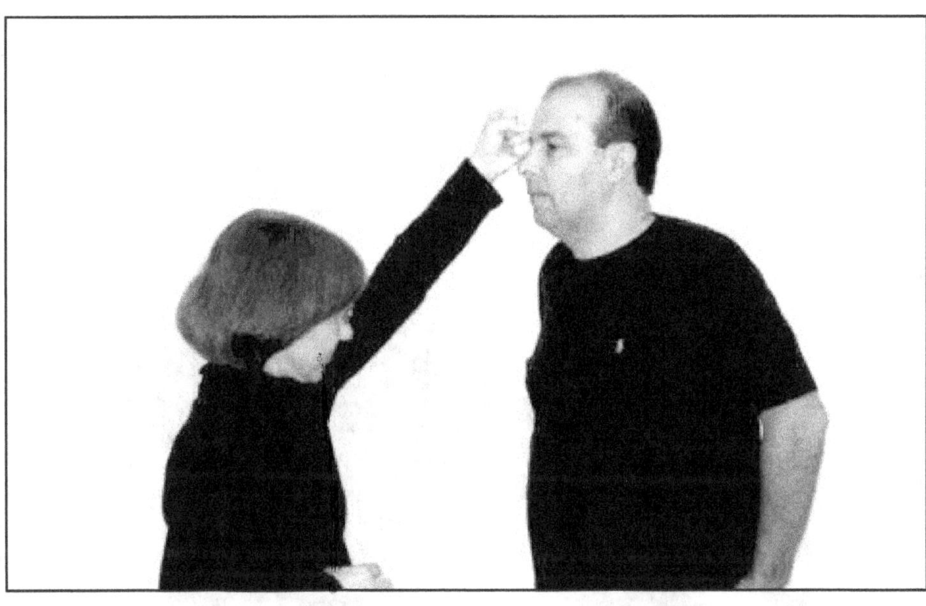

Closed fisted like this or open handed as above, this target area is easy to see, easy to hit, and effective in stopping an attack.

Breathing THE THROAT

Hammerfist to the Throat

The hammerfist is a powerful tool against a large assailant. This defender is in a position to run away from her attacker.

Hammerfist to the Throat

Notice the difference in the placement of the defender in this photo. Both the strike in the photo above and this strike contain enough power to kink the windpipe.

Breathing THE THROAT

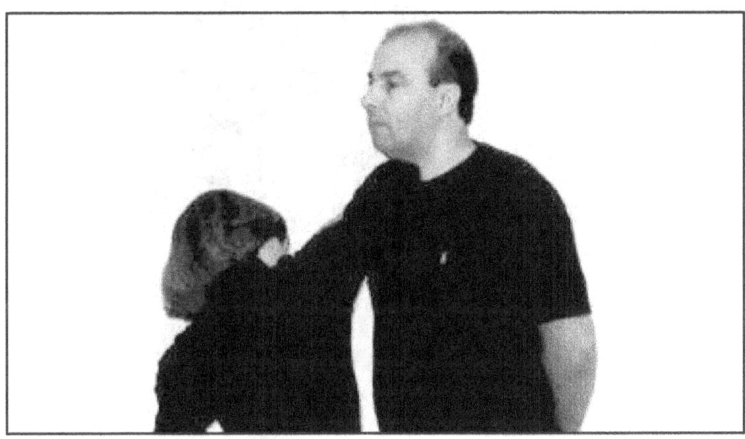

When you are close to the attacker, use your elbow repeatedly.

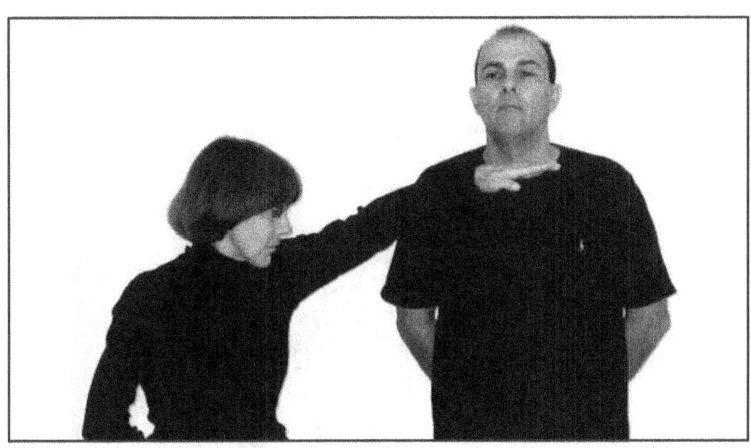

Here you see the knifehand striking the attacker's windpipe. Another great target is the side of the neck (no photo shown).

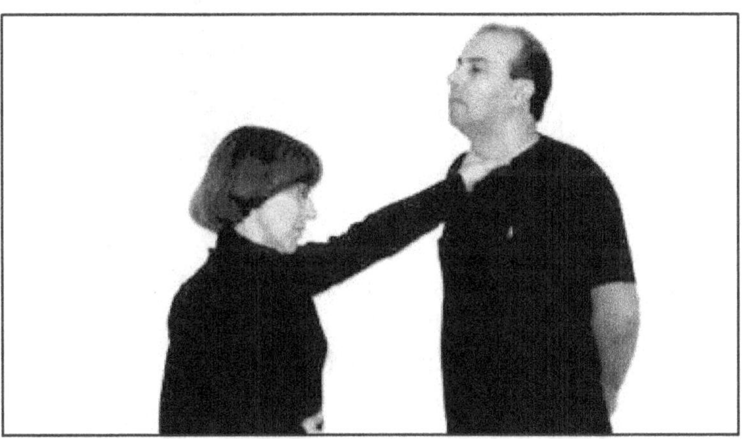

After you strike with the web of the hand, close the fingers around the windpipe to continue cutting off the air supply of the assailant.

Shock Absorbers THE GROIN

Kick to the Groin

When you kick to the groin, use your shinbone for maximum impact.

Knee to the Groin

Like the elbow, this strike works well when an assailant is very close. It also works best when you use it over and over, three to five hits repeatedly.

Fist to the Groin

Whether you use the thumb side of the fist or the hammer side, this is a great strike.

Another Use of the Fist to the Groin

I like this strike because you can open the fist, grab and wrench the groin area, causing maximum pain to the attacker.

Shock Absorbers THE GROIN

Umbrella to the Groin

Upper Left: Whether you use your hand, knee, or one of these tools, the groin is a prime target.

Bottom left: The upward swing of these weapons is easy to adapt to your self-defense strategy.

Bottom Right: I like the use of the hooked end of the cane. It adds to the pain that you will be able to inflict on your attacker.

Cane to the Groin

Another Use of the Cane to the Groin

Shock Absorbers THE SIDE OF THE KNEES

Kick to the Side of the Knee

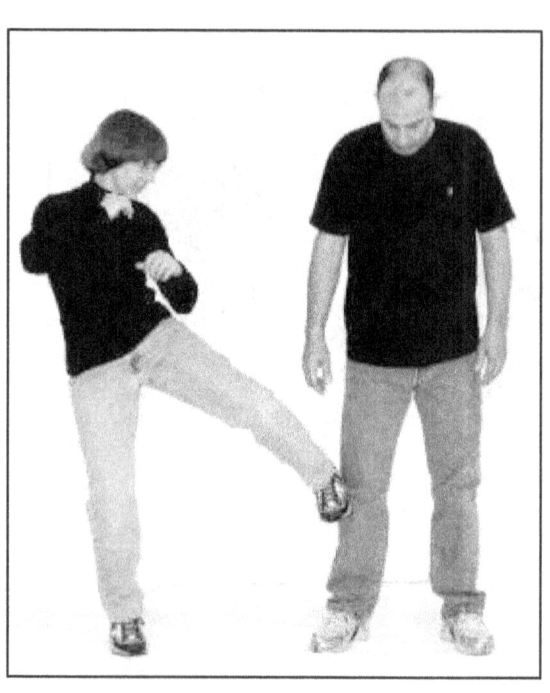

Upper Right: Keep your kicks below the attacker's waist. This will help you keep balance and maximize your power.

Bottom left: The front, side, and rear of the knee are great targets. Keep that thought in mind.

Bottom Right: All the available devices I have shown you increase your reach, making your defense practical and doable.

Umbrella to the Knee

Cane to the Knee

Shock Absorbers FRONT OF KNEES, A SERIES

Kick to the Knee - Begin a Series of Strikes

Upper Left: Start by driving the edge of your shoe into the front of the kneecap of the attacker.

Bottom left: Now slide your foot down the shinbone of the attacker. This will rake the skin free, causing maximum pain.

Bottom Right: A small defender can break the instep of a much larger assailant. Between the strike to the knee, the raking of the shinbone, and the possible breaking of the instep, most assailants will be thwarted.

Kick to the Knee - Continue the Series

Stomp the Instep - Finish the Series

Shock Absorbers THE REAR OF KNEES

Kick to the Rear of the Knee

Upper Right: Notice the proximity of the defender. Aim deep, hitting with a powerful part of your foot and ankle.

Bottom left: Where you strike the attacker will depend on your position when attacked.

Bottom Right: As I stated earlier, the front, side, or rear of the knee are all great targets. Your feet or a defensive tool are all great devices. Just hit and run for help.

Umbrella to the Knee (rear)

Cane to the Knee (rear)

Shock Absorbers THE INSTEP

Stomp the Instep

A small amount of pressure delivers a big punch when applied downward against the instep. High heels work just as well as flat shoes.

Cane to the Instep

This is an efficient use of the length and power of your defensive tools.

Interactive Exercise 8

Using the information we have discussed up to this point, think about these possible situations:

1. An attacker grabs your arm as you are getting into your car. In one hand you have your purse, in the other hand 2 bags. What is your plan?

   ____

   ____

   ____

2. You turn into your driveway, and for the second day in a row notice a car parked across the street. There is a man, on a cell phone, sitting in the car. What is your plan?

   ____

   ____

   ____

3. A stranger bumps your car with their car at a quiet residential intersection. You have to decide, right then, what you want to do. Talk about these situations with your workout group.

The Attacks

We're finally here. To the point where we will be able to hit someone! The assailant expects you to be unaware and unprepared. I cannot predict exactly how an attacker will surprise you. However, the techniques I recommend here will be useful in many situations. To strengthen your skill in defending yourself, practice by having a partner attack you. At first, having someone grab you is disconcerting. Working with partners will build your confidence. Use this text to create a strong foundation. But keep in mind that your individual thought, spontaneity, and willfulness should be the biggest factors in your defense.

The Attack is a Front Choke

Start with **talking.** Using both forearms, and fast full power, **hit your opponent's arms downward.** Even if he doesn't completely let go, the power of your hit will bring his face close enough to your hands for you to hit the "brains" as a target.

Next, use follow up strikes of your choice: we chose an **ear clap, knee to the face or throat and elbow to the spine.**

The Attack is a Rear Choke

Look! Talk. With arms bent, make a **half turn and hit your opponent's** arms with your forearms. Hit hard and quickly. Use your full body power. Never be distracted if the release isn't complete. You are in a perfect position to start hitting back.

Next, use follow up strikes of your choice. We chose a **palm heel strike to the face**. Finally, of course, **run**.

The Attack is a Wrist Grab

Note: There are many ways an attacker might grab your arm. I'll show you quite a few.

From the Front with Two Hands

To release a grab, **move your entire arm upward, as if you are going to point up. That move is toward the opponent's thumb**. In this grab, the thumb is located at the top of your wrist, near <u>your</u> thumb. The strength of your arm and the surprise will be enough to cause the release. Of course, **hit**! We chose an elbow. And **run**.

From the Rear with Two Hands

Look behind you and make sure who it is. Check their size and look for features to identify them later.

Use the same concept as above. Put the strength of your arm against their thumb. This will be easy because you'll be **pulling your arms forward**.

Strike back any way that is comfortable to you. We chose the very effective elbow.

Don't forget to **run.**

Now is a good time to mention that in order to defend against a wrist grab, it isn't necessary to make the attacker let go. The pictures below show a **shin rake** with foot stomp and **palm heel strike** to the face. I recommend this if the person is trying to drag you by your wrist. Use the close proximity and his pull strength, get close and start hitting. As stated many times. Hit hard, be accurate.

If you use this method, you can continue to **hit** to the face (brains) before you **run.**

We'll close up this section with some close up shots of the wrist. To review: the escape is in using your entire arm strength against the attacker's thumb strength. Remember that practicing these escapes with friends or your workout group will build your confidence.

In this set of pictures the attacker is using his right hand to grab across the body to your right hand.

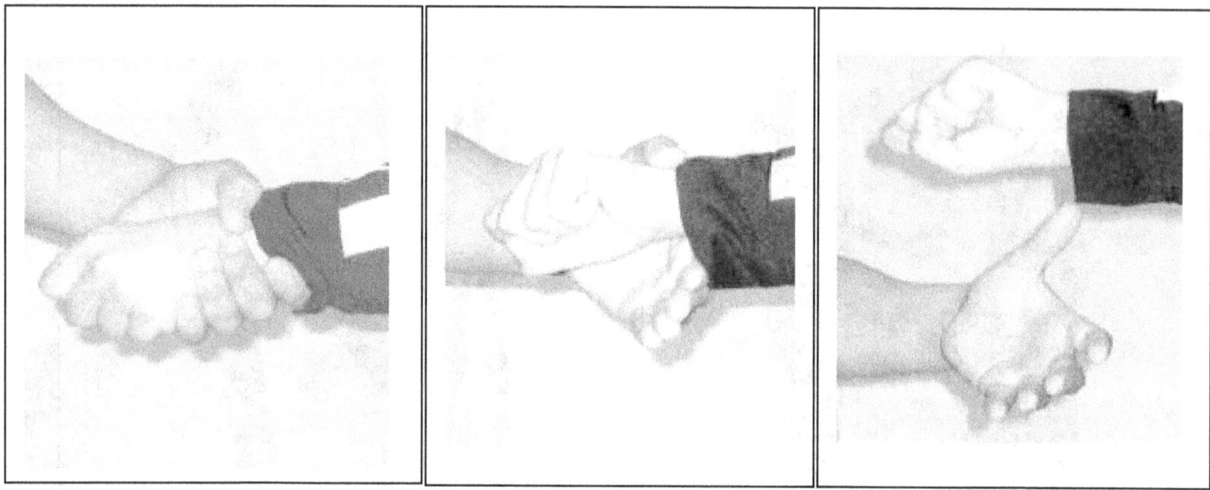

In this next set of pictures, the attacker grabs from the top, leaving the thumb opening on the bottom. Remember to notice where the thumb is located, to insure you're using your full arm strength against their weakest digit.

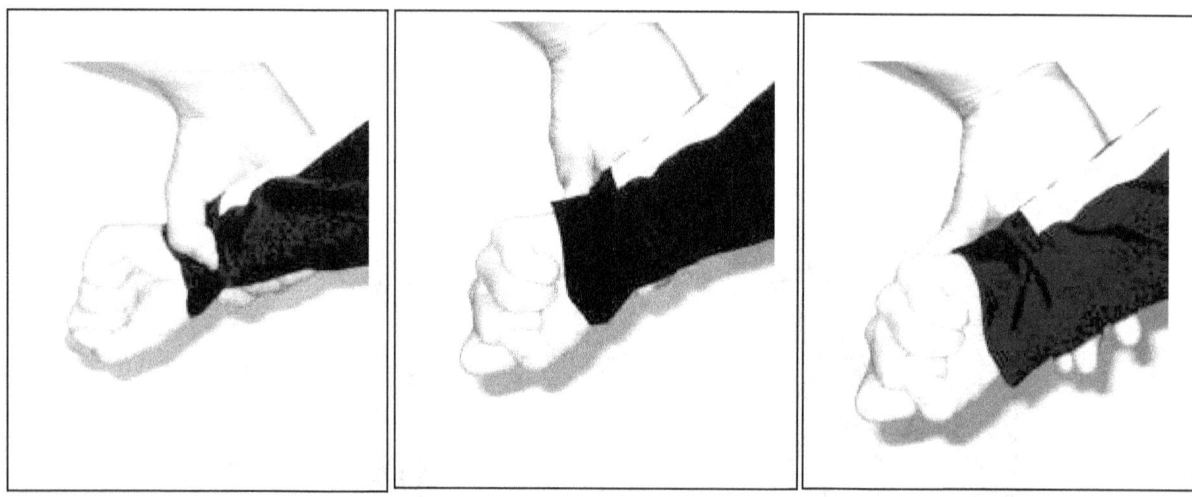

This last set of pictures depicts using the strength of both hands for the release.

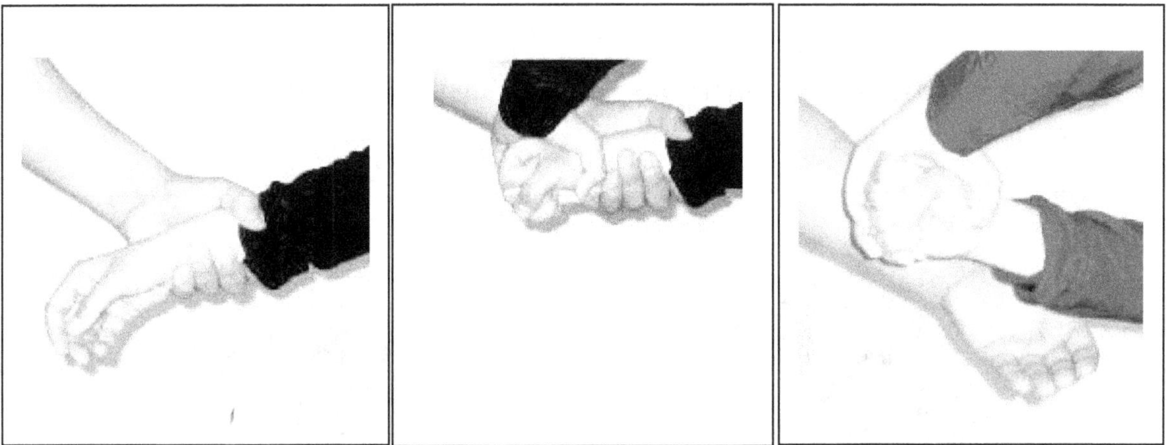

Please don't begin to feel overwhelmed. Keep in mind that an important part of this is to get together with a group of friends / workout partners and build confidence while having fun with these techniques.

INTERACTIVE EXERCISE 9

1. Talk to a friend or co-worker and create a practice session. Practice escaping from a front choke, rear choke, and wrist grab. Discuss with your workout partner how to improve your techniques.
2. With each practice session, increase the intensity of the grabs. Continue to discuss ways to improve.
3. Finally, have your partner grab you unexpectedly. Judge your reaction time and discuss plans to get stronger.

The Attack is a Front Bear Hug

Begin this series by **talking**. This might make the attacker look toward you. Then **use your forehead to break his nose.**

Next, rake the side of your foot down his shin and **stomp on his foot**. Remember, it only takes four pounds of pressure to break someone's instep.

This next step will take some practice. You'll want to **jab your knuckles** into their back at the edge of the bottom of the rib cage. Practice on a willing opponent, so you can understand the necessary aim and power. Need I say, **get out of there**, when you are free.

The Attack is a Rear Bear Hug

The rear bear hug creates the same impact as the front bear hug does. You might not see it coming, so remember that you will need to push through the surprise and shock. **Look** at the attacker. Talk to distract him. This technique is called a ski technique.

Start by **loading your hips forward** and pushing your arms toward your attacker. The technique is completed when you **drive your buttocks into their groin**, while driving your arms forward and upward. When completed, this technique makes you look like you are skiing, hence its name.

Kick the attacker in the knee cap. And/ or Hit with your elbow. Drive the elbow in with power, force, and a loud scream. It is time to **run**. Get away and get some help.

The Attack is a Variation of a Rear Bear Hug

This set of photos shows a common variation on the rear grab. The release used above will work for this attack. Start by trying to LOOK!

Raking the shin and stomping the foot will precede the 'ski technique'

Now it's time to repeat what we learned in the rear bear hug above. "Load the arms and hips. **Hit hard**. The follow up technique we use is the **kick to the knee**. Then, of course, Run.

The Attack is a Headlock From Behind

It is possible that the attacker might bend you forward with this attack.
If possible – try to LOOK and SPEAK. Perform the heel stomp you learned in the previous attack. Finally, **reach the hand closest to your attacker over his shoulder and stick your fingers into his eyes.**

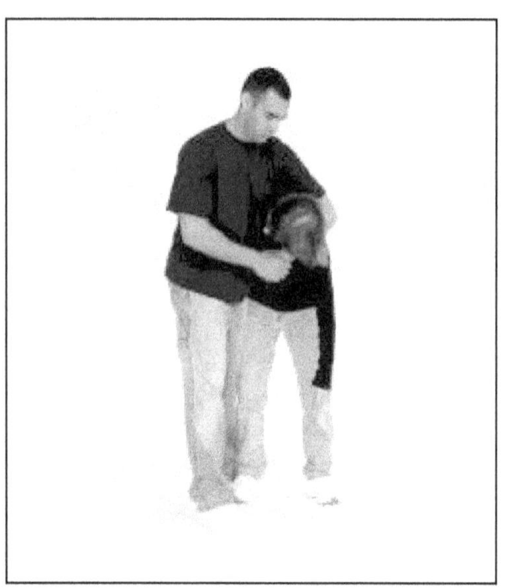

This technique can also be done by placing the edge of the hand on the upper lip. This version is not shown here. **Yank his head upward** and backward using the eye sockets. As he is being manually forced backwards, his grip will break.

As soon as his choking grip is broken, and using your other hand, **smash the windpipe**. The hammer fist strike is very effective during the defense. Do I really need to show a picture to remind you to **RUN**.

The Attack is a Variation of the Headlock From The Front

In this attack, you are being choked from the front. First apply a **strong hit to the groin with your forearm**. Fist your hand to make the muscles in your arm flexed and strong. Always strike the groin area in an upward motion directly between the two legs, not to the front of the groin.

Now **stomp the instep**. You will remember this from previous techniques. Running your foot down the shin bone increases the pain to the assailant. Grab the hand or wrist that is choking you. **Yank it downward**. As soon as you feel it begin to give way, start to rise for the next hit.

Use the familiar **elbow strike**. Hit the attacker anywhere he is vulnerable that you can reach: **temple, neck, jaw line, even the ribcage** will work. By now it is clear that I want you to **run**. Get away. Create distance between you and your attacker. Yell throughout the entire process.

The Attack is Someone Striking at You

In any situation where you think trouble is approaching, **get away**. You are not better off to wait for him to get close to you, as this victim is doing. As the attacker strikes at you, **put both arms up with muscles flexed as strong as possible**. When you are practicing this technique, I recommend that you put both hands up. That way both sides of your body are guarded and you are better prepared for the strike to come from either side.

Start your escape with a **groin kick**. Always hit with your shin directly between the legs for this kick. Try to kick so hard that you lift the attacker off the ground. A well placed **elbow** to the jaw should keep the attacker occupied with pain and his own defense.

Our defender uses a **second elbow** to finish the job. Since defender and attacker are in a face to face confrontation, the extra hit power will help. And now **run.**

Here's an idea: search for a partner or coach to practice blocking more often. As you have seen in movies and sports, moving your body as you block is the most effective. This requires some time with a boxer, karate teacher, or other expert in the field of fighting.

INTERACTIVE EXERCISE 10

1. Revisit the list of strikes that you like to use for your self-defense. Now that you are getting some hands-on practice, change the list as needed.

    ____

    ____

2. Practice escaping from all the new attacks. Assess your success. Are you starting with the negotiation and ending with the run for help?

    ____

    ____

3. Discuss your power, decisiveness and loud voice with your workout partner. Try to think of two ways to improve.
4. Practice blocking as your partner strikes at you. Discuss blocking. Do you find it difficult to flex the arm and make it strong? Do you automatically put up both arms? Do you keep your eyes open? Discuss ways to improve your blocking.
5. Make a short list of your favorite follow-up strikes. Hang it somewhere as a reminder.

Each chapter in this book builds on the one before. Please place this text in an area where you can review from time to time. I hope you enjoy the added confidence that practice brings to your daily life.

There is no magic answer for that moment when an attack surprises and shocks you. The method of defense will remain the same:

- Block
- Hit
- Run

CHAPTER 4
The Will to Act: Strengthening Your *Chi*

This chapter is one of the most important aspects of your self-defense plan. When you are in a confused, anxious, even scared moment - where defense is going to be necessary - how do you will yourself to act? How do you keep yourself from freezing up?

In karate, we believe that the willingness to take action will come when the person has strengthened their chi and learned to erase confusion and fear from the front of their thoughts.

This skill, like anything else, takes practice. Read this chapter and try some of the exercises. Seek more information by Googling "chi" and "ki". There are many books dedicated to this subject. If you are active in a karate dojo, ask your instructor for help and information on this subject.

What is *Chi*?

Chi is inner strength. This intangible power exists in everyone and is greater than just physical power. The Overlook Martial Arts Dictionary describes chi as "spirit or vital energy". This power is demonstrated at different times throughout the world. Seemingly impossible tasks are accomplished by seemingly ordinary people, when extraordinary circumstances present themselves. This is chi at work. Here are two examples:

A man runs miles on a broken leg to save his life.

A mother lifts a car to save her child.

One goal of a Martial Artist in training is to practice calling up this skill, thereby building confidence in this skill. This is not an impossible task. Like all skills, this one will take time, practice and a willingness to try and try again.

Where is *Chi*?

Every person has this power; it exists at all times. The most commonly accepted theory places chi in the abdomen approximately 1 inch below the belly button. Its exact location isn't as important as the concept that it does exist; and like muscular strength, is there to be utilized at will.

Drawing upon this power is nothing like flexing a muscle. In order for chi to grow, you must have an awareness of the energy and vitality that exists in you at all times. I fully realize that I am encouraging you to do something that is not easily defined. Don't let this lack of a tangible manifestation bother you. Recognize that chi is there and be willing to connect with it.

Now that I have described what chi is and where it is, I will discuss some ways to strengthen your chi.

Training

Karate training, by nature, builds chi. It is possible that one day you will call upon your inner strength for a simple task. (It might be something as straightforward as making a quick decision with a calm and confident manner, rather than in 'panic mode'). It will be there, and you can, with confidence, continue to rely on the knowledge that the exercises inherent in Karate training will continue to build chi. It isn't necessary to address your chi exercises as separate from your Karate training. As long as you are in training, your internal strength can grow stronger along with your physical body.

I will discuss a few exercises specifically designed to build and strengthen your internal power. These exercises can be used as a guide for anyone who is not presently training in a dojo and will serve as a supplement to those of you in training.

Meditation

I am reluctant to use the word meditation, as it evokes an image of Zen monks and stark self-denial. This state of austerity is not necessary for everyone. Random House defines meditation as "to think contemplatively". I like that definition. Try it. Sit quietly and contemplate. Here are some hints to help you begin:

- Take a position that opens the lower abdomen and allows full breaths. Poses include **lying** supine and **kneeling**. When kneeling, it is common to place a pillow between the buttocks and the ankles. This relieves any stress on the knees.
- **Consciously relax** the shoulders, jaw, back and forehead. Relax the entire body. Don't mistake relaxation with a limp spine. Visualize the body releasing tension. Start at the tip of your toes and travel to the top of your head. The spine should remain straight, the abdomen expanding with each in-breath and contracting with each out-breath.
- **Take air in** through the nose and allow air out through the mouth. Let each in-breath equal the time it takes to breathe out. Three, five, seven, even ten second in-breaths should take an equal amount of time to exit. As the air enters, the abdomen should rise, fill with energy. As the air is exhaled, the abdomen will flatten, essentially deflating.
- **Focus** by guiding your mind to a destination and hold it there.
  At first think only about breathing. Feel the air draw in through the nose. Consciously press the air into the lower abdomen. Release it from the abdomen as slowly and conscientiously as when you inhaled. Keep breathing and keep concentrating on the act of breathing. When your mind wanders (and it will), don't think about the fact that you lost focus. Go right back to breathing. Inhale. Exhale. This process will strengthen your ability to stay focused in daily life.

Below is a short list of obstacles that are counterproductive during meditation. <u>Don't:</u>
- Let your mind race.
- Let your breathing be shallow.
- Let tension exist in your mind or body.
- Let emotion (guilt, sorrow, excitement) play in your spirit.

There is no magic number of meditation minutes or hours or days that brings a person to better awareness. I like to tell people to try to take quiet, meditative time as often as it is possible. If you have two minutes, use them. Three minutes is good, five minutes will also work. Time is relative. Don't skip meditation because you are too busy. (Do you see the irony?) Any time spent sitting quietly with a calm spirit is time well spent.

Hints to help you begin:

Lay or Sit Quietly
Consciously Relax
Breathe deeply –in through the nose
and out through the mouth
Focus on just one thing

Things to avoid:

Frantic thinking
Shallow breathing
Physical Tension
Emotional roller coasters

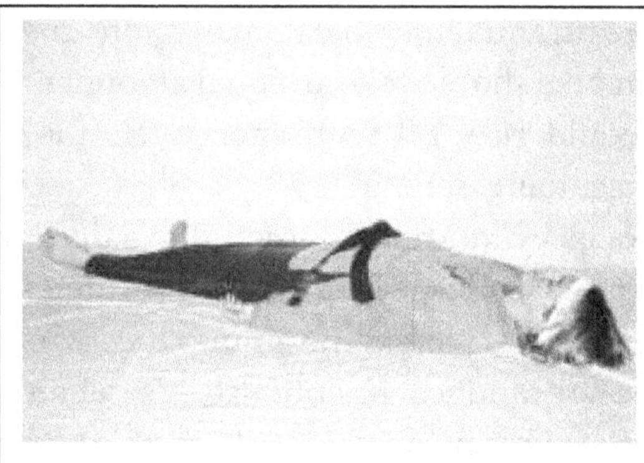

As you progress, you can change the focus of your thoughts. Again, this is personal; so don't be afraid to just follow your instinct (as long as you stay calm, breathe, and focus). Some common focus points in meditation include:

Color – just one clear and precise

Nature scenes – forest, sky, ocean

Ideas – honor, patience, benevolence, courage – just one at a time.

Remember, when you realize that you have lost your focus, don't let your mind linger. Immediately go back to the image you left behind. **Strengthen your ability to ignore distractions.**

Meditation should not be uncomfortable or burdensome. When you are finished, you should feel awake, alive, prepared and refreshed.

Chi Building Using a Partner

There are a few partner drills you can work to build your chi. The first one described here engages your muscles. Still, put your main focus on centering and engaging your chi pocket (the center of your abdomen, near your belly button). You and your partner will stand facing each other. Both of you should have your right leg forward, under your right hip and bent. Your left leg will support you from behind. Keep the left leg wider than your hips and very straight. This stance is called *Zen Kutsu Dachi*. You and your partner will have your right feet side by side. Place your shoulders close together, holding each other at the top of both arms. Your head should sit near your partner's left shoulder and your partner's head will do the same to your left shoulder. Both people will take a large in-breath, drawing the breath all the way to the abdomen. Breathing out from the abdomen, push against one another. The objective is to move the other person while not losing your balance. Try to place your power into your lower abdomen. Don't press from the shoulders. Exhalation should last 7 – 10 seconds. I repeat, try to keep your power firmly in your lower abdomen, not in your shoulders. At the end of the exhalation, stop. Let go of each other. Reset your poses with your left side forward and repeat.

- The goal is to strengthen your inner power – not to beat your opponent.
- Focusing on your opponent will distract you from your goal.
- Center your chi and go to work.
- Do not focus on the outcome. Whether the workout partner is bigger or smaller, it is completely possible to engage your chi, grow and become stronger.
- Stay grounded
- Keep your shoulders and hips in line. Don't let your upper body lean forward, possibly pulling you off balance.
- Breathe out with strength while working.

The next partner exercise is called Sticky Hands and it develops focus, perception and concentration. These three characteristics are helpful when engaging your inner strength. Start by standing, facing your partner. Make sure your breathing is coming from and traveling to the center of your abdomen. Put your hands in front of you at approximately the height of your shoulders. Have your partner do the same. Imagine that there is a sheet of paper between your hands and your partner's hands. Both your hands and your partner's hands are almost touching. One partner will use his hands to 'lead' by moving his hands slowly in different directions. The other partner tries to follow (stick to) the lead partner's hands without using sight. Do not follow with your eyes. Try to use your other senses. Close your eyes if it is possible. After 30 seconds switch who is leading and who is attempting to follow. Tension should not build up in the shoulders. Power should come from and return to the center of the abdomen, the chi pocket. Remember to keep your breathing centered throughout the exercise.

- Keep breathing deep into the abdomen, softly and consistently.
- Try not to use your eyes. Close them if you feel comfortable enough to do so.
- Switch back and forth who is leading and who is following.
- Keep your focus on the second that you are experiencing.
- Try not to focus on the concept of "beating" the opponent.
- Relax the muscles in the shoulders and back.

Both of the above exercises can serve as training tools. There is no magic number of repetitions recommended. Like the seated meditation, I suggest that you do what you can, when you can and let the strengthening begin.

Taking Risks

Taking small risks regularly is a way to build chi. Modern advertisements tout the idea that failure is NOT an option. The problem with this thought, as anyone who takes risks will tell you, is that if you take a risk you might not be successful. Are you a person who takes risks? Or do you walk away from these opportunities to guard against experiencing failure? When was the last time you spoke in front of a crowd, competed, or attended an event that made butterflies play in your stomach? If you do not do this regularly, try it.

I am truly sad that many people think of risk as something to watch others undertake, instead of something to experience. I am NOT advocating that you climb Mount Everest unprepared and alone. However, if that climb was something you were interested in, and you pursued it with logic, and strength, I am sure it would be worth it. How about climbing something close, realistic and a little less dangerous, but risky nevertheless? By doing something unusual you build your ability to cope in unusual circumstances. Defending yourself in a life-threatening moment will definitely qualify as an unusual and risky circumstance.

Conclusion

Chi exists in everyone. It will serve you well to be able to call on that added energy, confidence, and power. Strengthening inner power does not have to become a full time undertaking. Karate training and meditation will strengthen chi, as will competition and other risk taking activities.

My advice is this: Don't be distracted by the outcome. Enjoy the experience.

INTERACTIVE EXERCISE 11

1. With your workout group, discuss Chi and consider exercises that isolate and strengthen Chi.
2. Take a small risk and keep track of how you feel, before, during and after. Repeat this process as often as possible.
3. Make a note (written or electronic) to remind yourself to meditate – on a regular basis.
4. Play the "what if" game and measure your responses now, as compared to when we started this project. Is it quite different?

CHAPTER 5
Children and Safety

This is a subject that is near to all of us who love our children deeply. It is also a subject that is discussed, written about, and reinforced within this text, as well as in documents provided by churches, schools, and community centers. So, even though I'll reiterate a few of my favorite bullet points here, there is a plethora of information available for the safety of your children.

The Basics

Children need to be a part of their own safety from an early age. All the societal rules that keep women from properly being able to act in their own safety apply to children. Here are a few:

- Teach them to say what they mean and mean what they say. Teaching them will strengthen it in you.
- Teach them the difference between real danger and someone who is bothering them.
- Teach them to hit groins and feet and RUN.
- Teach them to yell loud while running.
- Teach them the simple escapes that you've learned from this text – Just in case.

I have discussed working directly with children on some aspects of their safety in earlier chapters. Here I'd like to go over basics that every child should learn as early as possible.

- Full Name
- Address, including city and zip code
- Important phone numbers

I suggest you create opportunities at home to remind children (of all ages) to remember these things:

- Don't answer the door when home alone.
- Don't tell people you're home alone.
- Tell parents where you are going, even if it is just in the yard to play, or to your friend's house next door.
- Have an escape plan for your house in case of emergencies.
- Have phones available to call 911 and make sure the kids know the situations that require 911.

It is a good idea to play games now and then to remind the children of these simple safety necessities.

Bullying

This is a world that children need to navigate. We should be aware of and take part in this aspect of their safety. My first suggestion is to research the subject. Start at www.stopbullying.gov . This site is informative. Although there is no one answer to the sad truth that people will forever try to push one another around, I'll leave you with a few pointers.

- Train yourself and your children to talk about what is happening in their life.
- Speak up at your child's school for their safety, comfort, and dignity. Most experts agree that the responses to start with are: ignore the bully, speak up for yourself once and if they don't listen, walk away from it and tell someone.
- Use all your senses for signs of bullying and don't be too shy or busy to speak up everywhere necessary.
- Be an example of letting people be who they are without cruelty or judgment. There is an old saying "Little pitchers have big ears." What we all need to remember is that, when children see us doing the behavior that is making them uncomfortable, their desire to be honest with us when it happens is lessened. Worse, they might copy our cruelty or sarcasm.

There is no better safety net for our children than our love, competent advocacy, and balanced approach to problems.

INTERACTIVE EXERCISE 12

1. Watch your own voice and demeanor in front of your children. Are you an example of the adage "live and let live"?
2. Work toward opening communication at a young age and keep it as open as possible.
3. Brainstorm, with other parents, the best way to act when bullying occurs.

Conclusion / Answers to Exercises

This text is a labor of love. I believe strongly that you can and should be willing and prepared to defend yourself, if the need arises. In order to make that idea a reality, you will need to be vigilant in your routine of self-defense readiness, as discussed throughout this text.

To that end, my conclusion chapter consists of reminders of pertinent information. I encourage you to make self-defense readiness part of your daily routine and live an active, safe life.

Answers to the Interactive Exercises

Exercise 1

1. Sit and consider our daily routine. Can you think of any parts of your routine that could use better safety precautions, awareness and readiness? List a few:
   - *Watching for unusual activity in my neighborhood*
   - *Have a routine that includes looking around when I enter and leave my car.*
   - *Keep my doors locked.*
   - *A land line if possible.*

   (There are many more that I hope you jot down.)
2. List situations that you have already thought of, where avoidance is a choice:
   - *Tell someone when I'm going out alone and when I think I'll return.*
   - *If I come home and see something odd at my home, stay outside and call for help.*
   - *Ignore rude drivers, walkers and shoppers.*
   - *Use the tip and watch to see if I'm being followed on foot.*
   - *Check parking areas before walking to my car. Park in well-lit areas.*
3. Define (in your own words) the four components of a complete self-defense routine:
   Pay Attention: *Keep my eyes open and live in the moment.*
   Be Prepared: *Have a plan "in case" and review it with friends and family.*
   Memorize Techniques: *Create a "workout party" to meet once in a while. Practice, eat, drink and laugh with my friends.*
   Willing to Take Action: *Make a note of ways to strengthen my chi from the chapter in this book. Practice them as often as possible.*

Exercise 2

1. What is worth fighting for?
   The only thing worth fighting for is your life and the life of your family. Things can be replaced. It is important not to mistake ego with justice when deciding to "stand your ground".
2. Take a moment to think of the places and times within your day that you might let your guard down and not take precautions for safety. List a few and brainstorm ways to increase awareness at these times:
   This is personal, so please really think about it! Here are a few of mine:
   - *When I'm at home and relaxing.*
   - *Driving and singing loud with the radio.*
   - *Anytime I'm on my phone.*
   - *When my arms are full of groceries.*
   - *I'm running late and rushing.*

Exercise 3

1. List at least three ways to keep the outside of your home safe.
   - *Keep the bushes by the front door trimmed.*
   - *Add a peephole to your front door and use it.*
   - *Know the neighbors, and pay attention when the cars in the neighborhood change.*
   - *Don't advertise that you live alone.*
2. Now list at least three ways to keep the inside of your home safe.
   - *Keep the doors and windows locked.*
   - *When people come to the door, check credentials before letting them enter.*
   - *Know what you have near each entrance to defend yourself, were it necessary. (pots, pans, spray cans etc.)*
3. Think, talk, or write about what your plan will be if you come home to an intruder.
   - *Dial 911.*
   - *Don't enter.*
   - *Fight ONLY if no other choice exists.*
4. List one household item in each room of your home that could be used as a weapon, if the need arises.
   The list is endless: flashlights, spray bottles (air freshener?) lamps, phones, kiddie toys such as bats, trays.
5. Name at least one way to empower your children in self-defense awareness.
   This depends on the age. In younger children make it a game. Practice self-defense techniques. Add lots of yelling. Speak without fear so they live without fear. The older

they get, the more detailed a plan can be, including when teens come home and realize someone has been in the house.

Exercise 4

1. Is self-defense outside the home very different than inside the home? Discuss:
    Not really. Both begin with Pay attention, Be prepared, and Be willing to do something.
2. Think of at least 2 safety precautions that you can use while traveling.
    - *Tell friends and family your plans.*
    - *Live in the moment: Pay attention to your environment.*
3. Think of the different stages of self-defense for your children. What applies at what age? Make a few notes for the future:
    Little children: Play safety games. Learn phone numbers and address.
    Age 8–10: Begin the discussion of what makes a danger. Continue to play safety games. Talk about safety when at home alone.
    Teens: Now it is complicated and includes traveling without the safety of parents, saying what you mean and meaning what you say, realizing that all people are not trustworthy, working techniques, taking safety classes, working and strengthening the will to act.
4. Phone a friend and discuss some of the ideas we've covered.

Exercise 5

1. What is your most important weapon?
    Your brain.
2. Define, "Say what you mean and mean what you say."
    It is important to be clear when I communicate. "Step back" is better than "You're standing too close." Think of more examples.
3. Discuss ways to make common sense safety a part of your daily life. Include places and times we might forget to implement these ideas.
    The Big 3 are:
    - *Pay attention to the moment you are in. Don't live distracted.*
    - *Avoid dangerous situations, rather than stumbling into them or inviting them into your home.*
    - *If danger strikes be instantaneously loud, strong and uber-confident.*

Exercise 6

1. List your favorite defensive strategies while driving.
    - *Keep doors locked.*
    - *Pay attention to possible dangers like being followed.*
    - *Look around in parking lots before getting out of the car.*
2. Name 3 common mistakes people make while they wait in a parked car.
    - *Forgetting to keep an eye out.*
    - *Forgetting to keep doors locked.*
    - *Getting out without looking around.*
3. Explain to a friend the danger of walking in the same direction as traffic is moving.
4. Play "what if" with these situations:
    - d.) An attacker grabs your arm as you are getting in your car. You have your purse on your other arm. What do you do?
    - e.) You drive into your driveway, and for the second day, you noticed a car across the street that you don't recognize with a man seated inside.
    - f.) A stranger bumps your car with his, just two blocks from your home.
      These are for you personally. Think about what you want to actually DO!

Exercise 7

1. The number or website of a gun safety course in your area is: _______________________
2. True or False: Acknowledging a stalker will fuel his behavior. *True*
3. List 2 actions you should take if you think you are being stalked:
    - *Do NOT contact the stalker.*
    - *Do report it.*
    - *Call a stalker hotline to reinforce these choices.*
    - *Have a friend keep an eye out with and for you.*
4. List conclusions that have meaning from the text so far. What do you want to remember?
   This is personal. Really consider what YOU think here.

Exercise 8

1. An attacker grabs your arm as you are getting into your car. In one hand you have your purse, in the other hand 2 bags. What is your plan?
   One idea is to drop the bags. Hit the attacker with your purse and run for help. You can also get into the car, lock the doors and drive away after hitting the attacker. There are many more choices. Think about what works for you.

2. You turn into your driveway, and for the second day in a row notice a car parked across the street. There is a man, on a cell phone, sitting in the car. What is your plan? *Call the non-emergency number for your police department and ask them to drive by and check it out. Discreetly take a photo of the tag/ car / man.*
3. A stranger bumps your car with their car at a quiet residential intersection. You have to decide, right then, what you want to do. Talk about these situations with your workout group! *Choose between these: Call a friend, or the police and keep them on the phone as you get out of the car. Or have the driver follow you to a less isolated location.*

Exercise 9 (These next few exercises don't require answers from me. They're hands-on exercises. Enjoy!)

1. Talk to a friend or co-worker and create a practice session. Practice escaping from a front choke, rear choke, and wrist grab. Discuss with your workout partner how to improve your techniques.
2. With each practice session increase the intensity of the grabs. Continue to discuss ways to improve.
3. Finally, have your partner grab you unexpectedly. Judge your reaction, time and discuss plans to get stronger.

Exercise 10

1   Revisit the list of strikes that you like to use for your self-defense. Now that you are getting some hands-on practice, change the list as needed.
2   Practice escaping from all the new attacks. Assess your success. Are you starting with the negotiation and ending with the run for help?
3. Discuss your power, decisiveness and loud voice with your workout partner. Try to think of two ways to improve.
4. Practice blocking as your partner strikes at you. Discuss blocking. Do you find it difficult to flex the arm and make it strong? Do you automatically put up both arms? Do you keep your eyes open? Discuss ways to improve your blocking.
5. Make a short list of your favorite follow-up strikes. Hang it somewhere as a reminder.

Exercise 11

1. With your workout group, discuss Chi and consider exercises that isolate and strengthen Chi.
2. Take a small risk and keep track of the how you feel, before, during and after. Repeat this process as often as possible.
3. Make a note (written or electronic) to remind yourself to meditate – on a regular basis. *Remember that one minute of quiet time will make a difference. Set an alarm in your phone as you begin to implement this strategy. It will improve focus and confidence.*
4. Play the "what if" game and measure your responses now, as compared to when we started this project. Is it quite different?

Exercise 12

1. Watch your own voice and demeanor in front of your children. Are you an example of the adage "live and let live"?
2. Work towards opening communication at a young age and keep it as open as possible.
3. Brainstorm, with other parents, the best way to act when bullying occurs.

Remember

Pay Attention

Have a Plan

Practice Your Techniques

Build Your Chi

Be Prepared

Look Around

Use Your Voice as a Weapon

Have a Potential Weapon in Your Hand

Everywhere

In the Car

At Home

While Walking

Always

Play "What if" Games

Have Your Favorite Strikes Ready

Practice Your Escapes

Recipe for Defense

Talk

Hit

Run

<u>Acknowledgments</u>

First, thanks to all the students who graciously posed for the many pictures. In order of appearance:

Lucas Mardis

Derek Pelatti

Lydia Ward

Bobby Nait

Angel Ortiz

Yolanda Gonzalez

Rudy Kerkerian

Wendy Schultz-Tallman

Lisa Drake

Jackie Kan

The work behind this book started in 1999 with the impetus of my student and friend, *Meral Ehrenstein* and her daughter, *Dorothy*. Then the work transferred to another friend and student, *Melissa Macy* with the unending help of *Jackie Kan* and *Tracey Broussard*. Here we are, with a finished copy that I truly hope makes people stronger and smarter about their own self-defense. Special thanks to *Chai Galapon* for her expertise in formatting, graphics and publishing. Finally, I'm forever grateful for the patience, support and perseverance of *Chai* and *Jackie Kan* throughout this process.

Md

2018